1D ONE DIRECTION

FOREVER YOUNG

OUR OFFICIAL **THE X FACTOR** FACTOR STORY

Foreword by Simon Cowell
Photography by Simon Harris

HarperCollins*Publishers*

Foreword by Simon Cowell

The decision to take five solo contestants and give them the chance to create a group was one of the best decisions we made. But the credit for making this group work goes entirely to Niall, Harry, Liam, Zayn and Louis, who embraced the idea and not only worked incredibly hard but became genuine friends.

The boys' attitude throughout the series made One Direction firm favourites with everyone both backstage and in *The X Factor* house. They are incredibly talented and hard working, polite and great to be around.

They've gone from being five young unknown lads to being mobbed wherever they go, and yet they've taken it all in their stride and remained as down to earth as when we first met them.

I can honestly say it's been a privilege working with them. They've taken everything we've thrown at them and run with it, they've brought their own ideas – whether it's been on their songs or staging – and every week they did an incredible job.

They know who they are as a band, the type of music they want to make and they are full of ideas and plans for the future. As their mentor, I was disappointed the boys didn't manage to become the first band to win *The X Factor*, but I have no doubt that they will go on to achieve great things and I'm very much looking forward to working with them for a long time to come.

The X Factor is all about discovering new talent, and One Direction are a testament to how much talent we have in the UK.

Thank you to everyone who voted for them and supported them throughout the competition. I know that they will not let you down.

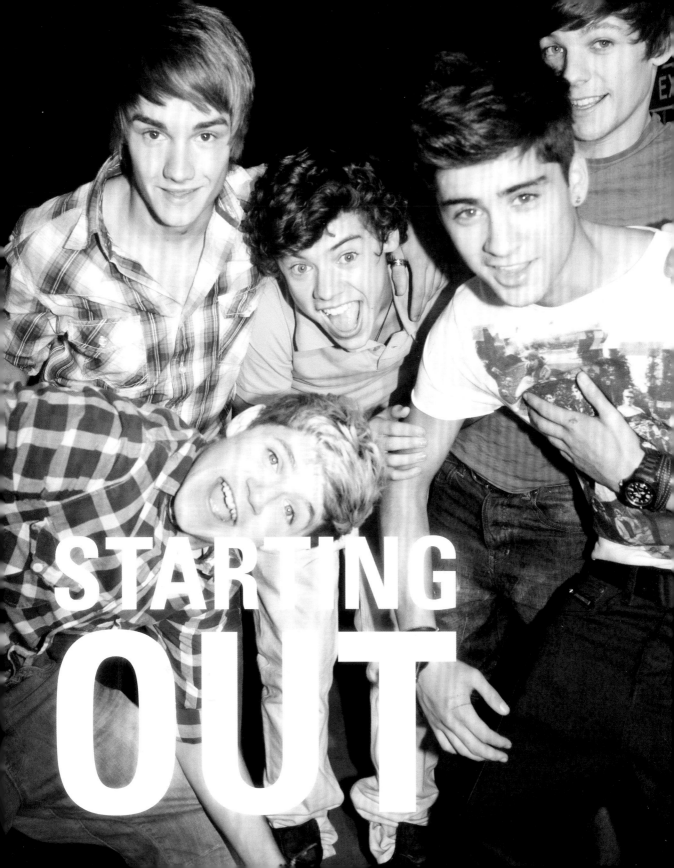

STARTING
OUT

In the beginning

Liam: I first started to sing when I was about six. We used to go to my grandad's in Cornwall or to holiday camps and I used to sing on the karaoke all the time. I loved singing Oasis, but my favourite track to perform was Robbie Williams's 'Angels'. I was in school choirs back home in Wolverhampton as well, and I went to a small local performing arts group called Pink Productions, so I was singing and also dancing.

I've got two older sisters, Nicole, who's 22, and Ruth, who's 20. I get on really well with them. They both like performing too, so we used to sing and dance around the house. That sounds a bit ridiculous, doesn't it?

I had a really nice upbringing. I come from a typical working-class background. My dad works in a factory, building aeroplanes, and my mum is a nursery nurse. I was planning to go and work in the factory with my dad, to do an apprenticeship, but my dad wasn't all that keen. He wanted me to sing! I was actually about to start the apprenticeship when I tried out for *The X Factor* the first time around, so the show kind of got in the way, but in a good way.

At one stage I wanted to become a boxer. I used to box three times a week, but had to give that up for *The X Factor,* as you can't turn up on stage with bruises. I was also the best 1500-metres runner for my age group in Wolverhampton and nearly ran for the country, so becoming an athlete was another career option. I liked the idea of becoming a fireman too. I've always liked helping people, so I was going to do the training course when I was 18. But although I was drawn to all of these, music was still my first love.

I was 14 when I first auditioned for *The X Factor* back in 2008. I made it all the way to Judges' Houses with Simon in Barbados and sang Take That's 'A Million Love Songs'. But Simon didn't take me through, because he didn't think I was ready for it. He said to me at the time, 'You need to go and get your GCSEs,' so that's what I did.

It was a terrible disappointment, but I was up against a lot of stiff competition. It was the year that Diana Vickers, JLS and Alexandra Burke were in it, so it was a tough year. And looking back, it was probably a good thing I got kicked out, otherwise I wouldn't be in One Direction now. I love being in a boyband and I think it really suits me. I also don't know how I would have handled something on that scale at 14. It would have been scary.

It was tough to go back to school afterwards, though, having been on TV in front of 16 million people. All of a sudden you're in a Spanish lesson you don't want to be in, so it's a bit of a comedown. Not that I ever got bullied because of the show. I was just always the boy who had been on *The X Factor*, so if anything it was cool.

For the next couple of years after my first audition I tried to make it on my own as a singer. I went through publishers and producers, but it felt like every time I was getting somewhere it fell through for some reason. You need a lot of time and money, and I wasn't living in London, which made it even harder.

I did manage to get some public appearances off the back of *The X Factor*, though. I'd be singing for 200 people one week, and for 30 thousand people at a football stadium the next. *The X Factor* definitely opened a lot of doors.

opposite page

Liam has been performing on stage from a young age

Harry: I grew up in Cheshire and I've got one older sister called Jemma, who is 20. We get on pretty well.

I was quite cheeky at school and got up to a little bit of mischief, but nothing too terrible. I liked to get my work done, but I also liked hanging out with my mates. I was good at English, RE and Drama, I think because they were the subjects I enjoyed most. All I ever wanted was to do something that was well paid. I could never really pinpoint what that would be, though. I really liked the idea of being a singer, but I had no idea how to go about it.

I started singing in primary school, and was always in plays and shows, so I was performing from a young age. When I got to secondary school I kind of stopped singing for a while, but later with some school friends I formed a band called White Eskimo. We performed locally and also won a 'battle of the bands' competition. Winning that and playing to a lot of people really showed me that singing was what I wanted to do. I got such a thrill when I was in front of people that it made me want to do it more and more.

When I went along to *The X Factor* audition, I was a student and I'd just finished my GCSEs at Holmes Chapel Comprehensive School. I had a Saturday job in a bakery and I was planning to go to college to study Law, Sociology and Business, but I wanted to see if I could make it as a singer first. If it didn't work out, then fair enough, but if I didn't try I'd never know.

My mum is always telling me I'm a good singer and it was she who put *The X Factor* application in for me. Obviously I was hopeful that the judges would like me as well. It would have been a major setback in my plans for world domination if they hadn't.

opposite page

Harry as a toddler

Niall: I grew up in Westmeath, in the middle of Ireland, with my parents and my older brother Greg, who is 23. We didn't get on when I was younger – I was probably a bit of an annoying younger brother – but as we've got older we've grown to like each other and now we get on really well.

As soon as I went to school I began singing. My teachers always said that I should join a choir, so I did exactly that. Then when I was nine I played Oliver in the school play, and that went down well, and I really began to enjoy being in front of an audience.

When I went to secondary school, everyone realised that I could sing, so I started entering talent shows and I even won a few of them here and there. I sang 'The Man Who Can't Be Moved' by The Script, and 'Last Request' by Paolo Nutini in two competitions.

While I was doing one of the talent shows, a guy asked me if I wanted to take part in a local *Stars in Their Eyes* type competition. I sang Jason Mraz's 'I'm Yours', and although I didn't win, I got a lot of good local press, which was pretty cool.

At school I loved French and Geography because I had really good teachers, but I was terrible at English and Maths. I talked a lot during lessons, but I didn't get into trouble too much. All the teachers seemed to like me even though I was far from the perfect pupil.

The town where I live is quite small and there isn't much for young people to do. I spent most of my time just hanging out with my friends or singing, and obviously all that singing is what led me to *The X Factor*.

When I went along for the audition I was a student at Coláiste Mhuire and I'd just finished my GCSEs. I was planning to go to university and study Civil Engineering, which would have been a bit different from the pop-star route.

Zayn: I've always been quite noisy and confident, even when I was a kid. I had bags of energy and I was always running around. In fact, I was so hyperactive that once my mum even took me to the doctor. I wasn't allowed any vitamin C because that's what was making me so hyper.

I was an in-your-face kind of kid and a bit of a handful. I always sang and I was in the school choir even in primary school, and then I carried on singing whenever I could. But not on the same scale as *The X Factor*, obviously.

previous pages

Niall practising his technique

Zayn with his older sister

opposite page

Liam loved singing from a young age

I've always been the loud one in my house. I've got one older sister called Doniya, who's 19, and two younger sisters, Waliyha, who's 10, and Safaa, who's eight. I like being the only boy because it means I'm pretty spoilt. I've got the big TV and a Playstation and they have to share a room, whereas I get my own.

I don't mean to sound like a bighead, but I was quite popular at school. I was a bit of a bad boy and I used to mess about and have a laugh. I did well all the same and passed 11 GCSEs with high grades. I remember my Drama teacher telling me that if I carried on and worked hard I could really make something of myself, but I thought she probably said that to everyone so I took it with a pinch of salt. When it came to A-levels I thought I could keep getting away with it, so I still messed about quite a lot, and I ended up with pretty rubbish grades.

I've acted since I was 12 and I've been in a lot of shows because I was at a performing arts school. I played Bugsy in *Bugsy Malone*, and was also in *Scrooge* and *Grease*. When I was younger, I always wanted to be an actor, but I also really liked the idea of becoming a drama teacher. Louis and I are very similar like that – he wanted to do the same.

I thought teaching would suit me. I come from a big family, as my dad was one of eight children, and I've got loads of cousins. We're always in each other's houses and I've always been around people. Also, I look after my younger sisters, and I like kids, so teaching felt like something that I could do.

Louis: I grew up in Doncaster and I talked a lot from a really young age. I've always been a little bit gobby and not lacking in confidence. Apparently I used to sit in my pushchair and talk to random people and get annoyed when they wouldn't reply. When I was about four, this man walked past and I said hello and he ignored me, so I turned round to my mum and said really loudly, 'He's mardy, isn't he?' I wasn't a shy boy.

previous pages

Zayn and Louis as toddlers

opposite page

Louis limbering up

I've got four younger sisters: Charlotte, who's 12, Felicity, who's 10, and identical twins called Daisy and Phoebe, who are six. I'm a pretty good older brother, I think. I get on really well with all of my sisters and I look out for them. People are often very surprised how good I am with kids.

I've always really enjoyed singing, but when I was younger I was much more into acting. I used to do little bits of work as an extra in TV shows like *Fat Friends*, and I also had a small speaking part in an ITV drama called *If I Had You*.

When I was about three I wanted to be a Power Ranger when I grew up. Then, like a lot of lads, I went through a phase of wanting to be a footballer. Since the age of 13 I've wanted to be an actor or a singer.

I always had a back-up plan, though. Because I love kids, I decided it would be great to be a teacher. There are so many teachers that are dead strict, so I wanted to be a fun Drama teacher. I'd planned my uni course and everything. It would have been funny if Zayn and I had somehow ended up on the same course.

When I was 14 I had a little spell in a band called The Rogue – great name! We did talent shows and put on shows at school and I used to really love it. That was what first made me think about auditioning for *The X Factor*.

I posted some clips on YouTube of me singing songs like The Fray's 'Look After You' when I was about 15 or 16, to try and get some kind of feedback. There's also a video on there of me performing as Danny in my school's production of *Grease*. I loved being in that show, it was such a laugh, and I was really pleased to land the role of Danny as it was the first show I'd auditioned for.

A lot of kids complain about school, but I actually enjoyed it and I really miss it now. It was more of a social thing for me, and I was always the one trying to make people laugh. The teachers either really didn't like me or really got on with me. I remember one of my RE teachers saying to me once, when I was about 15, 'I can tell by your personality that you're

opposite page

Harry dressing up

going to go on to do big things.' I went back to Doncaster recently and went to see his class and say hello, and he reminded me of it.

I did alright with my GCSEs, though, and got eight out of 11. I failed Business Studies, History and Geography. But then when it came to my A-levels I did too much messing around. Unless I love something, I'm not great at working hard at it, and I lost interest in my A-levels. Thank god for music!

The all-important audition

Liam: I'd always known I would give *The X Factor* another go, it was just a case of when. I never, ever gave up the idea of giving it another shot. Some people advised me against it – I think because they were worried that I'd get hurt – but most people were really supportive, which meant the world to me.

It was gutting to get thrown out the first time around. I knew how awful it felt and I didn't want to have that feeling again, but I was willing to take the risk. I wanted to get through more than anything. I had vocal coaching in-between so I could be at my best.

To me, that second audition was my chance to prove to Simon that I've got what it takes. I went there with one aim – to get a yes from him. Of course it also mattered to me what the other judges thought, but I guess because I had history with him I wanted to know that he felt I'd improved and moved on and grown up since he'd last seen me.

I knew that I could do well in the audition because I'd been working so hard, but there's always that danger that the nerves will get in the way, so the whole thing was pretty terrifying. Dermot calmed my nerves a bit backstage. He's such a nice friendly guy and when he recognised me, it put me at ease. He said it was nice to see me back, and I said it was nice to *be* back!

previous pages

Liam enjoyed his time at school

Niall on holiday

opposite page

Liam singing 'Cry Me a River' for his audition

Getting up on stage again was bizarre. I looked out and saw Louis, Cheryl, Simon and guest judge Natalie Imbruglia, and it felt surreal to be back there again. I just wanted to hear what Simon had to say. I really wanted him to say yes, for my parents as much as anything. My dad has always said to me, 'We'll get you on that show one day son.'

I sang 'Cry Me a River' because I had seen Michael Bublé perform it on TV, and within minutes I was on the internet trying to find a backing track I could practise along to. I wanted to do a really big song.

I got a standing ovation from the audience, which I genuinely wasn't expecting. I was close to tears when I looked out and saw everyone clapping and cheering. It was so overwhelming. Cheryl said to me, 'You've definitely got it, whatever it is, you've got it.' Then Natalie said, 'I think other people in this competition should be a little bit worried about you.'

Louis took the mickey out of Simon for not putting me through last time around, but Simon said he knew he'd made the right decision and that he felt I was a different person now. Not surprisingly, all of those comments made me feel very glad that I'd come back.

My family and friends were all waiting backstage, and they leapt on me as I walked down the stage stairs. Dermot gave me a big hug and joked, 'The boy becomes a man!' All I could think was, 'I've done it!' My face was actually hurting because I couldn't stop smiling. I never expected in my wildest dreams to get that kind of reaction from the judges and audience.

Niall: I'd always known that I wanted to try out for *The X Factor*. I think anyone in the country who sings wants to give it a go. It's the biggest talent competition out there, and this year felt like the right time to audition. I want to be like the big names in the world, like Beyoncé and Justin Bieber. I've been compared to Justin a few times and it's a comparison I like! I want to sell out arenas and make an album and work with some of the best artists in the world. I was hoping the audition day would be the start of it all. If I got through to the next round it was game on.

opposite page

After his first audition, Katy Perry tells Niall he is 'adorable'

I stayed with my cousin in Dublin the night before the audition but I didn't sleep I was that excited. I got to the Dublin Convention Centre at 5am and I was absolutely bricking it. There were so many people there, I thought there was no way I was ever going to get through. I even thought of changing my song at the last minute to improve my chances.

I felt so excited getting up on stage and singing in front of the judges, but of course the nerves were still there as well. Katy Perry was the guest judge and I had a bit of a joke with her about entering the competition so I could become more popular with the girls at school. It was half a joke, but half true, if I'm being honest.

I sang Jason Mraz's 'I'm Yours' and Simon said it was a lazy choice, so then I sang my other song, 'So Sick' by Ne-Yo. When I'd finished, Katy told me I was adorable, which are always the words you want to hear from a gorgeous, world-famous pop star, aren't they? But she also told me that I had work to do and that even though she'd started out when she was 15, she hadn't actually made it until she was 23.

Simon told me I'd chosen the wrong song and I wasn't prepared enough, but he still said he liked me, which was a massive bonus. Cheryl said no, but in the end I got three 'yes' votes because Louis more or less forced one out of Katy. That was enough to put me through to Bootcamp. Of course I would have loved the full four, but as long as I was going on to the next round I didn't mind too much.

Harry: Standing backstage with Dermot and my family before my audition was so surreal. All my family were giving me good-luck kisses, which was a bit embarrassing. I got some cheers when I walked out on stage, which felt great and made me feel a bit more relaxed.

I smiled and tried to look as confident as possible, but inside I was a right mess. This meant everything to me and I just wanted to do a brilliant job. There were hundreds of people there, but all I could see was Simon, Louis and guest judge Nicole Scherzinger looking up at me and I was like, 'Please like me, please like me.'

opposite page

Harry wows Pussycat Doll Nicole with his Stevie Wonder performance

Standing in front of all of those people was something totally new for me and I was really nervous. It was a big adrenaline rush and I think that's what gets you through the performance – you're on a bit of a high, so you don't really have too much of a chance to think about things.

I sang Stevie Wonder's 'Isn't She Lovely', a song I've always loved. I tried out loads of different songs beforehand and then chose the one I thought I sounded best on – which was that one, obviously! I even gave a little bow at the end, which was a bit cheesy, but I thought it would be funny.

Nicole said I had a beautiful voice, which meant so much to me, but Louis said I didn't have enough experience or confidence and that I was too young. Thankfully Simon disagreed with him and said, 'I think with a bit of vocal coaching you actually could be very good.' It was really nice to get the positive feedback. I honestly didn't expect to get through, so I was chuffed with the good comments.

Louis gave me a 'no', which was disappointing, but both Nicole and Simon gave me a 'yes', so I was through to Bootcamp. I was in a total state of shock! That was one of the best moments of my life.

My family went mad when I went back to see them. I was so incredibly happy, I didn't know what to do with myself. I kept expecting someone to come over and say, 'Actually, we've changed our mind, you're not through after all.' Can you imagine?

Zayn: I applied for *The X Factor* last year but didn't turn up for the audition because I was too nervous. I wasn't actually going to turn up this year either, but my mum basically grabbed me by the ear and told me I was doing it. It was something I'd always liked the idea of, and always thought I would do, but when it came down to it I panicked. So it took me a while to build up to it.

In the end I decided to go along to Manchester just for the experience, and if I didn't make it, then I didn't. When I got through the first stage and stood before the judges I thought I'd been kept so they could take the

opposite page

Despite feeling shaky with nerves, Zayn impresses the judges from the start

mickey out of me. I'd never had any singing lessons before and had only ever sung for my mum and my sisters or small audiences.

The day before the audition I went to sleep at four in the afternoon, then set off at two in the morning to get to the audition. My uncle drove me down, and he's nearly seven feet tall so there was no missing us in the queue.

I was really shaky beforehand and when I got out on stage I was suddenly faced by all these people. I had to take a deep breath to calm myself. There were people as far as the eye could see! And Simon Cowell was sitting in front of me; it was amazing but terrifying at the same time. I know he doesn't exactly hold back with the criticism, so I was really worried about what he would say.

I sang Mario's 'Let Me Love You', a song that I thought suited my voice and also one that I'd practised a lot. Louis said straightaway that he liked me, and Nicole said there was something special about me. Simon said he agreed with Nicole, but he also commented that I needed to be hungrier for it. I think Simon gets you as a person from the minute he meets you, and I think he was right – at that point I didn't yet want it the way I should have done, and he knew it. But the further I got into the competition the more and more I wanted it.

Louis: I auditioned in Manchester and I was one of the last people to try out. I first auditioned for *The X Factor* in 2009 but didn't get through, so I was determined to come back and try again. All I wanted to do was get to Judges' Houses. That was my target. I also wanted to know from the judges if I was any good or not. I wanted to have that experience so I could say I'd done it and not always wonder what it would have been like.

I thought about it all the time, so when I got the letter inviting me to auditions I was so happy. I wanted to work really hard and prove myself, and this time around I did a month's worth of singing lessons before I went along to my audition.

My best mate Stan came with me and we drove down on the Friday night before the Saturday audition. We set off at midnight, got to Manchester MEN Arena at 2am and, incredibly, there were already people queuing.

I set my alarm, got a couple of hours' sleep in my car, and then started queuing at 4am. Stan and I took our sleeping bags into the queue and we kept falling asleep, so people would nudge us and move us along every now and then. I'd already decided at that point that if I didn't get through on the Saturday I was going to sneak back on the Sunday and try again. I don't know if I would have got away with it, but I was willing to try.

I waited quite a while in the holding room, then my number was called. Just before you go on stage this guy counts you down and it's like, '3, 2, 1 – on you go!' As soon as I saw the audience and the judges, the adrenaline kicked in and my mouth went dry. I'd seen that scenario so many times on telly, and now there I was, in that place, with those judges. So much rested on that one moment.

I performed 'Elvis Ain't Dead' by Scouting For Girls, but Simon stopped me and asked me to sing something else, so I did 'Hey There Delilah' by the Plain White T's. Nicole made me feel a lot better by smiling at me all the way through, which was nice, as you never know what Simon's thinking. As it turned out, Simon did say he liked me and that I had an interesting voice, Louis also thought I had an interesting voice, and Nicole said something about liking how I looked. That was a surprise because my hair was pretty awful! The sides were really long and I had a bit of a mullet going on at the back. Thank god we got some styling done.

I got three 'yes' votes, but all of the judges said I wasn't confident enough, which may have been partly because I was so tired. If I ever audition for something again I won't do it on two hours' sleep.

Bootcamp and beyond ...

Liam: In July we all went along to Wembley Arena for Bootcamp. Obviously we didn't even know each other then, so to think we would go on to become a band is totally surreal.

Harry: There were 211 acts at Bootcamp in total, and when I arrived and saw so many people I didn't rate my chances.

Louis: Because Dannii was on maternity leave and Cheryl was still recovering from malaria, Louis and Simon were the only judges there at the start. On the first day, Louis told everyone, 'Bootcamp is tough. This is what it's all about. Showbusiness is tough. To survive in this business you've got to be tough.' It was all a bit scary. Suddenly everything seemed so real and we all had to fight to prove that we deserved to be there and to get through to Judges' Houses. I'd been having so much fun with the excitement of it all, but now there was everything to sing for.

Zayn: Simon also gave us a pep talk telling us how the competition could change our lives. When he said that one of us standing there was going to win the competition I was like, 'Oh my god, that could be me.' Then I looked around and knew that everyone wanted it just as badly as I did. I had no idea how good everyone was, but they must have been alright if they'd got to Bootcamp, so I was going to have to work harder than I ever had in my life.

Niall: Louis said they were looking for a star and they were only going to pick the best people. Half of all the contestants were being sent home on that first day, so it was pretty scary. By the end of that very day it could have all been over for me and I could have been getting on a plane back to Ireland. Needless to say, that was the last thing I wanted to do. Having got that far, I wanted to go all the way.

Harry: We were all put into our different groups and that's when I first met some of the other One Direction lads. Each category was given a song to sing and we got Michael Jackson's 'Man in the Mirror', which is a great track. The judges said that they wanted everyone to sing the same song so they could judge them just on vocal talent and not on the song choice, which made sense. But it also meant that somehow I had to put my own stamp on it. I was up against a lot of other guys and we were all trying to stand out, so it was tough.

previous pages

The contestants prepare themselves for Bootcamp

'I was preparing to go home every time there was a cut, and I knew how horrible it was going to feel.'

Zayn: I like competition, it's good. But when I heard the other guys who were in my category, I thought they were absolutely amazing. I don't have the highest voice in the world, so a Michael Jackson song wasn't the easiest for me to sing. I thought it was going to end for me there. I was preparing to go home every time there was a cut, and I knew how horrible it was going to feel. I was so happy when I got through on that first day.

Liam: I think that goes for all of us. Funnily enough, Niall and I shared a room at Bootcamp and we got on really well. We had a laugh and sang songs together. We were practising a lot too, but there were long days with a lot of work, so when we got back to the hotel, most of the time we just wanted to chill out and have a laugh. We also became friendly with Cher at Bootcamp. Oh yes, and apparently I then went out with her, but that never actually happened.

Louis: I got friendly with Aiden and Zayn pretty quickly after we met on the first day, and I was also mates with a couple of other lads. I spent a lot of time with a guy called John Adams, and he and I spent most of our spare time rehearsing. We knew we didn't have the strongest voices of all the people there, but we didn't want to come out of the competition thinking 'What if I had rehearsed a bit more?' We worked really, really hard.

Niall: It was a real laugh staying at the hotel, but it got totally wrecked one night. It wasn't us though, honestly. I was fast asleep at the time it was happening. I remember someone kicking the door of my room at about two o'clock in the morning and it woke me up, and then the next morning when I left, there was broken glass and mess everywhere. I know who was responsible, but I'm not telling.

Harry: When we arrived for day two and Simon told us that they weren't making any more cuts that day, I was so relieved. He also said that he could see a star in every category, which got everyone feeling really excited. Then he dropped the bombshell that we were going to be taught how to dance. There were some people that you could already tell were amazing dancers, so I panicked a bit. I've done a bit of dancing here and there but I had no idea how I would handle a whole routine.

Louis: Brian Friedman told us that we were going to be learning a proper routine. My mouth just fell open. I had no idea what I'd be like but I was willing to give it a go.

Zayn: I was absolutely horrified. I cannot dance to save my life. A lot of people were from dancing backgrounds and had experience, but this was a totally new thing for me and I wasn't getting it at all. I found it so frustrating and it made me feel like I didn't want to be there. I know that sounds bad, when I had this great opportunity, but I felt really self-conscious in front of everyone.

Louis: We were all dancing to Lady GaGa's 'Telephone' and I remember Simon noticing that Zayn was missing and asking if anyone had seen him. I didn't think for a moment that he'd done a runner, but it turned out he'd left the stage and gone backstage to sit it out.

Zayn: I seriously didn't want to take part because I hate dancing. I'd never done it before and I just felt like an idiot. I was on stage with people who were far better than me and I just felt ridiculous. I thought I'd mess it all up. Some of the other people there were professional dancers and choreographers and I was totally clueless. I felt embarrassed in front of Simon and everyone. So I decided to go and sit backstage and hope that no one noticed.

But they did. Simon came to find me and he wasn't happy. He told me I was wrong to bottle it, and he pointed out that if I didn't give it a go, I'd never be able to do it. He basically said I should try it or I'd be messing things up for myself, which made sense. In the end I thought I might as well just give it a go, no matter how stupid or uncomfortable I felt. Simon was right – how else would I learn? He told me never to do something like that again and we shook hands on it, and I went out to join everyone else.

I obviously need to practise my dancing skills and try to polish them up a bit, but I did alright. I need to dance in front of people more and just try to be more confident, because in this industry it is important to be able to dance. And I'm definitely getting better. I don't think Justin Timberlake is going to be panicking about losing his dancing crown, but I'm not too bad.

Liam: I thought the dancing class was fun. I used to be in a dancing group when I was younger, so I'd done choreography before, but to be in something of that level was great. There were some absolutely amazing dancers on the stage, but I love the fact that everyone gave it everything they could. I just went for it and it was brilliant.

opposite page

After trying to escape the first dance lesson, Zayn starts to gain confidence

Niall: Before we left for the day, we were given a list of 40 songs and we had to pick one to perform the next day, then go away and practise it. Louis warned us that this was our last chance and not to mess it up. No pressure then! I chose 'Champagne Supernova' because I'm a big Oasis fan and I thought no one else would sing it. I was right as well – I was the only one at Bootcamp who chose that song.

Harry: Liam and I both sang the same song, 'Stop Crying Your Heart Out'.

Zayn: And Louis and I both sang 'Make You Feel My Love'.

Louis: I think at that point every single person there wanted to get through more than they had ever wanted anything in their lives. We were days away from potentially getting through to the Judges' Houses round. Simon then reminded us that of the 200,000 people who auditioned, we were the final 100. It was incredible to think that.

Harry: You could feel how nervous everyone was the next day. Although the other days had been pretty tense, something was definitely different and everyone seemed much more hyped up. I felt a bit sick with nerves all day. Now it was so close, I wanted to get through to Judges' Houses more than ever. When Simon told us, 'Today will be the most important day of your lives,' he had a point. I thought I was going to pass out.

Niall: Simon told us that Nicole Scherzinger was joining them to make the final cuts, and when she walked in we all started clapping. She was absolutely stunning. She told us it was time to separate the men from the boys and the pussycats from the dolls, which was pretty funny.

Harry: I was the first of the boys to audition, so that was a bit of added pressure. And we all watched each other too, which made it even worse. I put absolutely everything into it, then all I could do was wait to hear my

opposite page

Niall and the other contestants wait nervously for what could be their final performance

fate. As you go through Bootcamp you kind of appreciate how big the prize is, and it made me realise more than ever just how much I wanted to stay and make it all the way to the live shows.

Liam: I was shaking before I went on stage to perform. I was still clutching my lyrics seconds beforehand and making sure I knew them inside out. Having such a good first audition is a brilliant bonus and I was still buzzing from it even then. But it's also a negative thing getting great comments because it meant that I felt like I had so much to live up to and the judges were expecting so much from me. When I did my initial audition it was almost like I had a whole year to work on it and decide on my song and practise a million times. But for the final Bootcamp performance I only had 24 hours.

I'd messed things up a bit in rehearsals, which put me even more on edge, because in that situation there's no such thing as starting again. There was only one thing on my mind, and that was to prove to Simon that I meant business and I wanted to go in there fighting and show I had what it takes. As soon as I got on stage, I told the judges, 'The reason why I think I've got *The X Factor* is because I had a knock-back at an early age, I took on a huge challenge, I set myself a goal and I never gave up.' Then I just went for it.

Harry: We all knew that the next few hours could determine the rest of our lives. Everyone was feeling really emotional, and after I'd sung I kept going over my performance and thinking whether I could have done it better and what the judges may have thought. It was hard not getting feedback, because it meant we had no idea how we had done.

Niall: When I found out that they were taking eight acts through from each category instead of six, I was thrilled. It was only two extra people, but I might have been their seventh or eighth choice, so it could have been my break.

opposite page

Liam awaits his turn to show Simon that he means business

Louis: I remember being interviewed by a camera crew and they asked what I thought my chances were of going through to Judges' Houses. I said, 'Only eight people are going through, and there are eight better singers than me out there so I don't rate my chances.' The guy interviewing me told me I sounded as if I didn't want it, but that couldn't have been further from the truth. I just didn't want to build myself up too much if I was then going to be let down.

Liam: The moment when we were all called to the stage, everyone looked terrified. When the names started being read out, everyone was barely breathing as they waited to see if theirs was called.

Zayn: The more names they called out, the more I thought I was going home. And when they got down to calling out the eighth name, it was awful because all the boys who were left on stage were praying it was them. When it wasn't me, I felt totally crushed.

Harry: I was so gutted not to make it through. You're standing there hearing other people's names being called out and then yours isn't and it just feels awful. When it got to the seventh person it was like, 'Oh, there's one place left. I've got no chance.'

Niall: That's the worst thing I've ever had happen to me in my life. I was standing there waiting for my name to be called out, and then it wasn't. I was so upset. I had a feeling I wasn't going to get through but it didn't make things any easier. I was already planning to come back the following year.

Liam: When I found out I wasn't through, the first thing I thought was, 'I just don't want to have to go back home and tell people I didn't make it.' As soon as I came off stage, I phoned my parents and told them the news. I was so gutted. We'd all worked so hard, and my parents are always helping me with everything and paying for things and they believed in me so much. So I felt I'd failed and let them down.

Louis: I was disappointed I didn't get through but I wasn't shocked. I was a lot more shocked that Harry and Liam didn't get through. I was like, 'What the hell?' I didn't even expect to get through the first audition if I'm being honest, so anything else was a bonus.

Zayn: I felt terrible. After having got so far, it was gutting to have not made it to Judges' Houses.

Harry: We were all really upset and trying to deal with the prospect of having to go back to our normal, everyday lives after such an amazing experience. Then the five of us were called back for what they said were 'interviews'.

Niall: Harry and I were already sitting outside with our suitcases, ready to go home, when they came and got us. We were sitting on the concourse of Wembley Arena feeling miserable and thinking it was all over.

Louis: After being called back, we were standing together backstage. We looked over and some of the camera crew were talking about how they were going to film that section, so I did have a feeling that something was going on. Then someone said that they wanted us five lads on the stage because the judges had an announcement to make.

Niall: I was so stupid that, even though we were five young lads standing together in a group, it never occurred to me that they might be thinking of putting us together as a band. It was funny because even though there were loads of people there, we'd all spoken to each other earlier that day at some point, and I'd shared a room with Liam in the hotel, so we kind of knew each other a bit.

Harry: We were chatting about what could be going on, and then we were told to go up on the stage. When we walked up, the Belle Amie girls were standing there looking just as confused as we were.

Liam: When Nicole told us that she thought we were too talented to let us go and they wanted us to form a group, my head started spinning. She said, 'You're going to get the chance to see what it's like to be a group.'

'I don't think any of us knew what to say. It was like things were moving in slow motion.'

Then Simon told us that they'd decided to put us through to Judges' Houses and that we had a real shot at the competition. I don't think any of us knew what to say. It was like things were moving in slow motion. It was so unexpected.

Louis: All of a sudden the reality of what she said kicked in and we started going mad, jumping up and down and hugging each other. I was crying like a little baby. Thank god we had all met that day otherwise it would have been like, 'Hi, who are you? Oh, we're in a band together.'

Niall: Simon said he'd given us a lifeline and he expected a lot in return. He warned us that there would be ridiculously long hours, but we didn't mind one bit. Just to have that feeling of being given another chance was unbelievable. Every time I think about it, even now, I get a bit of a shiver, and it's one of those moments that I will remember for as long as I live. And probably longer. Simon said to take five minutes to think about it, but I didn't hesitate. I was like, 'Yes, without a doubt.'

Louis: I was exactly the same. For me it's 'act first, think later' and it was just such an amazing opportunity.

Harry: I was the same. I was in from the word go. It was a choice of going home with nothing or making a go of something that could turn out to be amazing. I didn't even have to think about it.

Zayn: Me neither. I just knew we'd have a brilliant time together, whatever happened. I'd got on with all the lads when we'd been hanging out and I really thought we could make it work.

Liam: I had to think about the band thing for a bit longer than everyone else because I'd been there before and I'd been trying so hard to do the solo thing. I had to decide whether I was ready to throw all of that work away. But saying no would have meant throwing *everything* away. I'd have gone home with nothing. I'm so glad I made the right decision. I don't think I was ever going to say no, but I was worrying about how it would work. Niall lived in Ireland, and I didn't have a clue what all of the others sounded like, so I was throwing myself into something having no idea how it would be. But now it's turned out to be the best thing ever. Being able to phone my parents again and tell them I'd got through after all was amazing. It was one of the best moments of my life so far.

Niall: As soon as we all decided we would go for it, we immediately started talking about things like what clothes we were going to wear. I said we should all look like Louis because at the time I thought he looked really cool. How wrong I was! Only kidding.

Harry: We didn't get to celebrate that night, as most people headed home, but we were excited as hell about meeting up again. I don't think I've ever seen five people smile as much.

Louis: We really wanted to gel as a group and rehearse as much as we could before Judges' Houses. Harry's stepdad had this bungalow in the grounds of his house, so we all lived there for a week after Bootcamp and it was great. It was like student digs.

Niall: The work really kicked in then, and that's where we all kind of came together and bonded as a group. It hit us all that we were a band and we formed a really strong connection.

Zayn: While we were there, Harry came up with the name One Direction – because we were all going in the same direction as a group. Funnily enough, it was the first name we came up with, and we were like, 'Brilliant, we'll go with that one.' But it wasn't the only option. Another name we thought of was USP, and Liam's dad came up with Status Single, which was just awful.

opposite page

Harry shows his excitement at getting through to the next stage of the competition

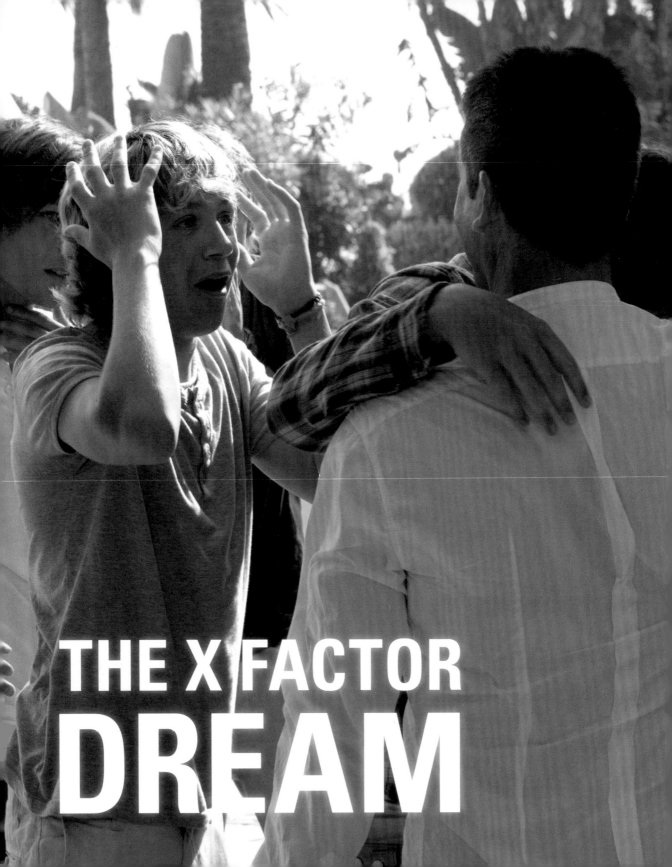

THE X FACTOR
DREAM

Judges' houses

Harry: The other boys headed home for a few days after being at mine and then we all met up again at the airport when we were flying out for Judges' Houses. We were all buzzing and really excited about going to Spain together, because we knew we'd have a laugh. We'd also been working really hard, so we felt pretty well-prepared for the audition.

Niall: For some weird reason I was certain from early on that Simon was going to be our mentor. I just had this feeling. He'd put us together and had said that the groups were really strong. But when we got to the house and saw what it looked like, I thought maybe we had Cheryl instead. I just thought it was a 'Cheryl' house. Then, after looking around more and seeing how lavish it was, I decided it was Simon after all. It was so funny, because the house was really near a public beach, and if the people walking past had known what was going on in that house they never would have believed it.

opposite page

The boys can't believe their luck that Simon is their mentor

Louis: I had a feeling our mentor was going to be Cheryl. So when Simon walked out, Niall was like, 'Told you, Louis!' Obviously we were well happy that we had Simon because he's the main man in the music industry, but I wouldn't have been disappointed if it was Cheryl either. Not only is she incredibly hot, she's a lovely woman and great at what she does.

'It was amazing when Simon walked out and we knew we'd got him. We all went mad.'

Liam: I was so happy to get Simon as our mentor because I knew I had an understanding with him. When we got to Marbella I had an inkling it was him, and Niall was adamant, so I think I ended up convincing myself it was a definite. It was like a lads' holiday out in Spain, and we had such a good time and bonded more than ever. But we did work really hard as well, and we practised as much as possible. We had no idea if we'd get through but we gave it all we could and did our best.

Harry: It was amazing when Simon walked out and we knew we'd got him. We all went mad, and the next moment we were laughing our heads off when he said, 'You had that dreaded thought it could have been Louis, right?' We would have been happy with any of the four judges looking after us, but I think secretly everyone wants Simon to be their mentor.

Niall: Judges' Houses was one of the funniest times of my life. We all shared a room in this hotel and there was this massive window in it. We used to open the window and then shout things out of it to people below and they'd have no idea where it was coming from. It was ridiculous, but so funny. Louis also threw a pizza into the swimming pool, which I thought was really funny, but Liam told him off. Bad Louis.

Zayn: It was brilliant because we got to go out a bit as well. We went and got pizza, and we also messed around on the beach, which was wicked. It felt like freshers' week for the band.

Louis: It wasn't all good, though. I ended up in A&E just before we were supposed to be performing for Simon, because I got stung by a sea urchin. I was in the sea and I thought I'd either grazed my foot or got a bit of stone in it because it was bleeding. I slept on it, thinking it would be fine, then I woke up and it was double the size of the other one. I went to stand on it and fell to the floor. That was when the pain kicked in and I had to go to the doctor's and have a jab in my bum, which almost made me faint. I was sick afterwards as well.

this page

Louis refuses to let his painful foot affect the band's performance

Harry: It was the day of our performance so we were worried he wouldn't be back in time, but thankfully he was. We would still have given it our best shot, but it wouldn't have been the same.

Louis: When we had to perform, I limped over to where we were singing and Simon was laughing at me. It was a nightmare, and I was really worried it would make it difficult to move around, but I battled through the pain and it was fine in the end.

Zayn: We sang Natalie Imbruglia's 'Torn', which was the song we were given. The performance went well, but afterwards we were chatting and we couldn't work out if it was a good thing or a bad thing that we'd only just been put together. I suppose the good thing is that we were quite fresh and we had raw talent, but we didn't have that knowledge of what it was like to be in a group for a long time. We were just unsure about what would happen and if we'd done enough.

Liam: Some of the other bands didn't like us, because they thought it was unfair we'd been put together and we were in their category. But it was always going to be competitive, so we didn't worry about it. And we generally got on with everyone, which made it even more painful when it came to finding out who had got through.

Harry: We had practised so much and worked so hard, and we were really sure of the song, so we felt very, very happy when we came off stage. We got so into it that we actually felt deflated when we came off because we wanted to be back out there again. But we still had no idea what Simon and Sinitta actually thought of us. We were one of the last two groups to find out, so it was between us and Princes and Rogues. Your hunger for it grows and grows as you get through each stage of the competition, and it's just the biggest stage at which to be told yes or no, so we were all in a panic. If you get a yes, it's one word that will change your life for ever. And if you get a no, it's straight back to doing the kind of stuff that probably drove you to be there in the first place.

Zayn: We were supposed to be the first to be told whether we were in or out, but then they changed it and we were told we were third. Then in the end we were second to last, so we had all of that time to wait to find out, which was the worst bit. We were coming up with all of these conspiracy theories: 'Are we being made to wait because we are getting through? Or is it because we aren't getting through? Is it good or bad that we're having to wait?'

Liam: Standing in front of Simon and waiting for the verdict was awful. When he finally talked to us, he said some positive things and some negative things, so we still had no idea which way it would go. When we got a yes, we went crazy. We were so, so happy. We all went and jumped in the pool with our clothes on. We just went for it.

Louis: I couldn't go in the pool because of my leg, so I just had to watch all of the fun. I did get to join in the fun on the flight home, though, and we had a great laugh. We were on such a high and just couldn't believe we were through to the live shows. When we got home we stayed in contact by phoning and texting, and then it was time for us to move into the contestants' house.

Going live

Niall: When we first got to London we stayed in a hotel for a few days because the contestants' house wasn't ready. There were still beds to be put together and things like that.

Harry: When we finally got to move into *The X Factor* house, it was really exciting. We'd been waiting ages for it to happen. Living in the contestants' house is great if you're in a group because if you have any problems or, on the flip side, if you're up for a laugh, you've got four other lads to turn to. We'd all bonded quickly and become brilliant mates, which was just as well, as we ended up sharing a room. It would have been absolutely no fun if we hadn't got on with each other. Our bedroom was pretty much exactly what you would expect from five teenage lads. It was an absolute tip most of the time, with clothes on the floor and unmade beds. We were a bit of a cliché. But Louis was without a doubt the messiest.

Liam: It wasn't the biggest room in the house and we had bunk beds, so we felt like little kids again. Also, Harry snores and we had to tell him off a few times.

Zayn: We could have got a bigger room in the house, but we're not complaining because we had such a laugh and we were enjoying every

minute of it. We got given a list of rules – things like 'you must keep the house tidy'. Obviously they soon went out of the window.

Louis: It was basically like sharing a room with your four best friends. There was loads to do in the house as well, so we were never bored. We hung out in the beanbag room a lot, playing Wii or table tennis. And we had a lot of takeaways. A lot. It was loads of fun, but even so, I did miss home sometimes. I think we all did.

Niall: I didn't. Gary Barlow always says that his favourite time of year is when he hasn't seen anyone for ages, then he goes home for Christmas. That's the way I look at it too.

Week 1

Liam: We were practising so hard in the run-up to the first live show. We had a really good song, Coldplay's 'Viva La Vida', which we all really liked because it was a bit different and not what anyone would expect from us. Even Simon said that it wasn't a song you'd ever connect with a band like us, but he said that, strangely, it worked. And if anyone knows, he does.

Louis: We put in loads of preparation and then we just couldn't wait to get out on the stage and show everyone what we could do as a group.

Harry: So much hard work had gone into it, that now we were all really excited and couldn't wait to be on the stage in front of a massive audience.

Louis: It was important for us not to think too much about what everyone else in the competition was doing. We needed to focus on our own performance. At the end of the day, if we did our best, then hopefully the public would see that and they would keep us in.

Zayn: We got a makeover in Week 1. The hair stylist, Adam Reed, said he wanted to give us a bit of a Burberry feel, which was cool. We were all really open to ideas, as long as they didn't give us perms or dye our hair pink or something.

Louis: We were trying to go for a really current, fashionable look. Mainly to impress the ladies. Thinking back, my hair did look a bit ridiculous at Judges' Houses. It was too long and just chucked to the side, but I thought it looked good. How wrong I was. Then Adam came to the rescue and we found a great picture and based my new hairstyle on that.

Harry: With the makeover we all kept our own individuality, but we needed to look like a band as well, so we kind of got twists on the looks we already had.

Niall: My hair was brown with stupid highlights before, but it got changed to bleached Eminem blond. I'm not going to lie, it hurt my scalp. I don't know how women do it.

Zayn: Finally, on 9 October, we got to sing live on TV for the first time. It was absolutely mad. There had been such a build-up, so we just wanted to get out there and kick it.

Harry: Being through to the live finals was just incredible. Even more amazing than we expected.

Zayn: We were all feeling so nervous, but maybe me more than anyone. When we had been practising the song with Savan, the vocal coach, I was actually out of time. Obviously I couldn't afford to make a mistake like that on the live show. That one mistake could have ruined it and ended it for us all.

Harry: On the night, the performance was amazing. Walking out and seeing the audience and knowing how many millions of people were watching us was crazy. But we loved absolutely every second of it. What a buzz!

Liam: We got amazing feedback from the judges. Dannii told us it was a perfect pop-band performance, and Cheryl said she thought the girls at home would be going crazy for us. But she also said we needed more time to develop as a group, which was a fair point, looking back. We hadn't been together that long, but we were getting stronger all the time. It was in that first week that we were most worried about going home.

Zayn: We didn't know what was going to happen and whether the public were going to take to us, so it all rested on that first performance and how people voted.

Harry: You're either going to be liked or disliked or somewhere in the middle, and that first week is the big decider. We were so relieved when we went through.

Week 2

Zayn: We loved performing in Week 1 – it was incredible, as Harry would say. And we loved getting to meet loads of the fans. They are amazing.

Harry: Week 2's rehearsals weren't all plain sailing, though. At soundcheck we'd only just begun singing and, when it came to the bit where I sang, I started feeling really ill. I felt like if I'd sung I would have been sick. I didn't understand it. I'd never had stage fright that had actually prevented me from performing before. It was really strange.

opposite page

Louis enjoys being given his new image

Liam: That week was difficult for us, because Harry is a big voice and a big character within our group. But we all auditioned for this competition as solo artists, so if Harry hadn't made it to the performance, we'd have had to step up and carry on without him. You have to play the cards you're dealt.

Harry: Thankfully, I was eventually given the all-clear in time for the Saturday, but I was still feeling a bit rough on the day, if I'm being honest. The other lads really looked after me and I was still looking forward to doing the show. We were performing Kelly Clarkson's 'My Life Would Suck Without You', which is such a cool song.

'We loved performing in Week 1 – it was incredible, as Harry would say. And we loved getting to meet loads of the fans. They are amazing.'

Zayn: Luckily, on the night we all pulled it off and it felt even better than the previous week.

Louis: The audience were amazing too, they were really behind us.

Niall: When it came to the judges' comments, Louis said that he thought we'd all gelled together really well, which was true. Surprisingly, considering how long we'd known each other, we were already like five brothers. I know it's a bit of a cliché but it's true. We got on so well from the word go and we were always having a laugh.

Louis: Cheryl called us heart throbs, which really made us laugh. And made us very happy. Like Louis, Cheryl made reference to the fact that we were close and said she knew we would have looked after Harry when he was ill, which we did. We were always looking out for each other, right from the word go.

Liam: Cheryl also said she was looking forward to hearing us do a big ballad, and to be honest we were really looking forward to doing one as well, so we were hoping we'd get to sing one the following week. Being on stage is absolutely amazing. We only spent a short time up there each week, but we wouldn't have changed a second of it.

Louis: We were absolutely loving working with Simon. People think he's really scary and intimidating, but he's just like a normal guy. We'll stand backstage and have a chat with him. We can always talk to him about our performances and music, but we also talk to him about football and girls and things like that. He's really supportive and very hands-on, and as well as being a good mentor, he's a great bloke to have a bit of banter with.

Week 3

Louis: We got a real taste of fame in Week 3 when we had a trip out to Topshop.

Zayn: I've never seen so many people. It was hard just getting into the shop, but we loved it. There were so many amazing fans there.

Harry: We got to choose a free outfit, which was great. Free things are a massive perk of this job, without a doubt.

Liam: I went out when we had a day off and I got free ice-skating. I also bought some cheap tickets to see *Oliver!*, but when I got there the guy recognised me and gave me tickets for these amazing seats instead. For free!

Harry: Our song for Week 3 was a little different from what we'd done in the past two weeks. We were doing Pink's 'Nobody Knows', so Cheryl was going to get her wish to hear us do a bit of a ballad. It wasn't actually our first choice of song, though, so there was a last-minute panic to get it rehearsed and right in time.

Liam: We had to work very hard and get on with learning the song so that we could get it right. Simon, though, had total faith in us and said, 'It's not will they, won't they? They'll just do it. They'll deliver it.' And I really think we did. We loved being able to do something different.

Niall: We loved our group performance that night, Cee Lo Green's 'Forget You'. All the group performances were a good laugh. Doing Corona's 'Rhythm of the Night' was pretty cheesy but very funny. We used to really look forward to them each week because it was a chance to let go and just have a crack.

Harry: After we performed 'Nobody Knows', Louis said we were like five Justin Biebers, which is never a bad thing because look how successful he is. He's huge. Then Cheryl likened the hysteria around us to The Beatles and we were like 'Wooooaaaahhhh!' That was just amazing. I mean, how many bands have had that said about them? We made sure we didn't get too big-headed, but we did high-five each other afterwards.

Louis: Cheryl Cole performed that week and she was amazing. We all had a little crush on Cheryl.

this page

Liam and the rest of the boys are thrilled when Louis Walsh compares them to Justin Bieber

opposite page

Harry gives his voice a well-deserved break

Liam: We met some amazing girls on the show, but I was gutted that Leona Lewis didn't come on because she's my big celebrity crush. She's my ultimate type. I love curly hair, but I hate lip-gloss.

Harry: I like girls with short hair, so Frankie Sandford from The Saturdays is my ultimate.

Louis: I like Pixie Lott. And Hayden Panettiere is amazing. I don't really like girls who wear too much make-up.

Niall: My crush is Cheryl. I know that sounds predictable, but she is unbelievable. I like girls with dimples, and girls who are funny.

Zayn: I just like naturally pretty girls, simple as that. I don't really have a type. I don't think you can tell until you meet someone.

Liam: Harry is the biggest flirt in the band, though, without a doubt. He's terrible. That's kind of his role.

Louis: I'm not really like people think I am. I know I'm a bit mad sometimes, but I do work hard and I make sure things get done, so I *can* be sensible. Liam and I are probably the leaders in a way.

Liam: Yes, Louis does have a laugh, but when we need to work, he'll work. It will usually be Louis and me kicking people up the backside when we need to crack on. We sort of work together as a team. But Niall just loves to have a laugh 24/7.

Louis: His memory is terrible. He's like a goldfish.

Niall: That's not fair.

opposite page

Louis enjoys his time in
The X Factor house

Harry: Oh, it is.

Louis: Harry is like the balance in the middle. He'll mess around but he will work. He knows where the line is. If there's ever a band argument, he's the peacemaker too. On camera Zayn is quite shy, but in real life he's not like that at all. He's come out of his shell so much.

Zayn: The funny thing is, I've always been quite loud. But for some reason on TV it seems like I'm the quiet one. Probably because this lot are so loud.

Liam: I'm the one who is 24/7 serious. Well, 23½/7. When it comes to work, anyway. I think it's because I've been trying to do this for so long that I'm so keen for it to work. I messed about the first time round in *The X Factor* and I didn't rehearse enough, but now I've got a second chance I'm not going to blow it, and I want us to make it in a big way.

Week 4

Zayn: We went to the London Dungeon in Week 4, and that was a real laugh. Niall was such a wimp about it because he got scared.

Niall: It was pretty scary, like!

Liam: We're so lucky that we're in a band, because if we'd gone there on our own it wouldn't have been as much fun. We have a laugh about absolutely everything.

Harry: We've all had little arguments in the band here and there, but it's more like a sibling thing. We'll bicker, but then we'll get over it really quickly and move on.

Louis: We also went to see Tinie Tempah at Koko in Camden during Week 4, with Cher and Mary, which was amazing. We got to meet Kimberley Walsh and Nicola Roberts, who were lovely to us. Then Tinie called us all up on stage, but while we were going up, I tripped over something and twisted my ankle. It was really annoying that I hurt myself, but I just had to get over it and keep going. At the end of the day I still had to perform and just hope it was alright on the night. It would have taken a lot more than a twisted ankle to stop me getting up on that stage, though. In the end I strapped it up tightly and took painkillers and it was fine. It just hurt a bit afterwards.

Harry: We were so excited about Week 4, especially after getting such amazing comments from the judges in Week 3. For us to keep proceeding in the competition, we had to get better each week. The theme for that week was Halloween, so we were wearing this fake blood and red eye make-up, which should have been a bit ridiculous, but it really worked.

Zayn: We sang 'Total Eclipse of the Heart' that week, which some people thought was a weird choice, but we loved it. I think it paid off too, because it was probably one of the best songs we did over the weeks.

Liam: It was nice to sing a song that everybody knows. We knew that everyone at home would be singing along and loving it. In previous weeks we'd done songs that weren't all that familiar, but this was brilliant.

Harry: We wanted to show that we could make big improvements in a week and keep getting better vocally and performance-wise.

Liam: Louis admitted that he had been worried about our song choice, but that actually it really worked. He also said that a lot of people had been asking him about us, which was another massive boost. Then Simon told us what a pleasure it was working with us. It was one amazing thing after another. He said it was easy to forget that we were only 16 and 17.

opposite page

It's easy to forget that the boys have only known each other for a few months

To be honest, we don't even give it a second thought, but I guess we are pretty young to be doing all of this.

Zayn: We were disappointed when Louis said that Simon was favouring us over Belle Amie. It was a bit harsh because it made us look like the bad guys.

Harry: It felt as if our hard work was being devalued. We were really shocked that Belle Amie went that week, but it showed us once again that we had to up our game. We knew that no one in the competition was safe.

Zayn: Us being in the band still felt almost unbelievable. Liam said one day that it all seemed like a dream and that we were going to wake up and our mums would be there shouting 'Get up, you've got to go to school.' And that's exactly how it did feel. I still couldn't get my head around the fact that we were performing to millions of people each week.

Louis: It may have been easy for people at home to look at us and think we were just having fun at that time, but the reason we were having fun is because we were working so hard. Working hard meant that we did well in our performance each week, and that in itself made us feel amazing.

Week 5

Louis: As the weeks went on, things did get scarier and scarier. You never know how long you're going to be in the competition for, and you're always so desperate to stay, so it was hard knowing that every week someone had to go. When you've got through on the Sunday you're over the moon, but then someone else has to leave the competition. You want to jump up and down and cheer, but then you see someone else's journey ending in a second and it's so hard.

opposite page

The boys perform Kim Wilde's 'Kids in America' for American Anthems week

Zayn: Sometimes we found ourselves feeling rubbish even though we'd got through. Like when Aiden went. We were all really angry about that because he was our mate. You get so close to everyone living in the house and it's like a little family.

Simon picked a brilliant song for us in Week 5: Kim Wilde's 'Kids in America', which is a classic. We got to have a load of cheerleaders on stage with us as well, which was pretty cool.

Liam: We all agreed that it was the most fun we'd had so far on *The X Factor* stage. It was great when we did 'Viva La Vida' the first week, but this topped it.

Harry: I think it worked well for us because we were able to have so much fun on stage, and hopefully it made us more entertaining.

Niall: The competition was very, very strong this year, so we were pleased that we showed a new side of ourselves. Once again, Louis gave us great feedback and said we reminded him of Take That, Westlife and Boyzone. But he did have a bit of a pop at Simon, saying that our song wasn't in keeping with the theme, American Anthems. He even called him a cheat, which was a bit unfair.

this page

Harry prepares himself for the red carpet

Louis: Cheryl fought our corner, though, and said that we'd brightened up her night, which was brilliant. We wanted to put a smile on people's faces when we went out week after week.

Week 6

Harry: We got invited along to the Pride of Britain awards in Week 6. It was such a special evening.

Zayn: We met some absolutely amazing people and it was properly inspirational.

Louis: Cheryl got a custard pie in the face and came back about five minutes later looking flawless. Only *she* could do that.

'He said to us, "It's quite weirdly thrilling for me to meet you all because I have been watching you every week." We were like, "Daniel Radcliffe watches us!"'

Liam: It was incredible being there and I was in tears at one point. Gary Lineker also told me off for flirting with his wife, Danielle. I'd met her down at the show a couple of weeks before and told her she was beautiful. She must have told him and he came over and went, 'I believe I need to have a word with you about flirting with my wife.' Then she came over and kissed me on the cheek and said, 'This is my new boyfriend!' It was brilliant.

Niall: We also went to the Harry Potter premiere that week, so we got to walk down two red carpets in one week! And we got to meet Daniel Radcliffe. We were all sitting down in this room waiting to go into the premiere and suddenly, with no warning, Daniel Radcliffe walked in. It was amazing. He said to us, 'It's quite weirdly thrilling for me to meet you all because I have been watching you every week.' We were like, 'Daniel Radcliffe watches us!'

Louis: Of course, I had to ask the question everyone wanted the answer to – 'How fit is Hermione?' Daniel said she was very fit but she was like a sister, to which Harry replied, 'Not to me she's not!' Daniel then told Harry he could fantasise all he liked. Harry was very happy about that. Emma Watson was my first proper crush when I was a kid.

Niall: We all have a crush on Emma Watson, so getting to meet her was incredible. She was so sweet, and we saw footage of the show afterwards in which she said we were gentlemen and that she was going to vote for us. Result!

Liam: Let's not forget that Niall fell asleep in the cinema. We had to wake him up because we didn't want anyone to catch him. How embarrassing would that be?

Louis: The theme for Week 6 was Elton John songs, and it was a real challenge for us. We were out of our comfort zone because we're not that familiar with Elton's back catalogue. But our aim was to improve constantly and we were happy with our song because it was a brilliant ballad, 'Something About the Way You Look Tonight'. It was a proper love song and different from what we'd done so far in the competition. Expectations were high, and we wanted to continue to fulfil them.

Liam: We love a challenge and Simon knew that, so each week he pushed us that little bit harder. He kept telling people that we were going to be there until the end, so we wanted to work as hard for him as he did for us.

Harry: After we'd sung, I loved hearing Louis say, 'I think after that performance you're only going in one direction, and that direction is the final.' We all wanted to jump up and down and shout. Then Simon said that he honestly thought, for the first time ever, a band could win *The X Factor*. I mean, it doesn't get better than that, does it?

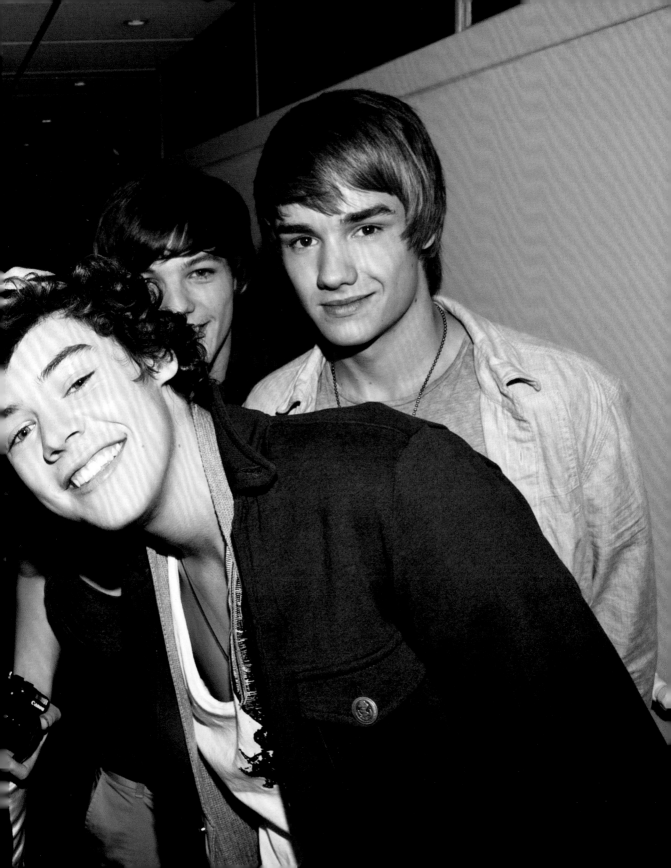

Niall: That week, Take That, Westlife and JLS all performed, and it was brilliant getting to see them. We had a great crack with the Westlife boys. They gave us some sound advice – be who you are and don't let it all go to your head – which is what we plan to do.

Louis: We saw Take That perform and I got to talk to Robbie and have my photo taken with him, which was wicked as he's my absolute idol. We met JLS as well and it was mad to think that two years ago they were on the show in our situation and now they've done so well. It was really inspirational seeing how far they'd come.

Harry: Elton John week was incredible all round. The crowd were absolutely brilliant and it was probably the biggest reaction we'd got out of the audience so far. And of course we got through again on the Sunday, which was also amazing. We were very sad that Aiden went home, though, as he was one of our close friends.

Zayn: We were all really close to Aiden and we missed him a lot.

Week 7

Harry: One of the highlights of our weekends – apart from the performing of course – was seeing our families. We always got to see them after the show and it's nice to relax, have a drink and spend some time with them. Loads of my family came along in Week 7.

Zayn: We also got to see the celebrity performances over the weeks. Nicole Scherzinger was amazing, and Michael Bublé was just like a normal bloke and really friendly to us, which Niall loved as he's a massive fan. The Wanted were nice lads as well. We hung out with them and were chatting like mates.

opposite page

Harry poses with Cher and *The X Factor* stylist Grace

Liam: We did often get to see the celebrities when they came on. Their dressing-rooms were along the corridor where we lined up before going on stage, so they'd often come out and say hello. We didn't see a lot of Usher, though, which was disappointing.

Louis: We did get to meet Katy Perry though and she was dead funny. I love her music.

Harry: Everyone thinks that it's all glamorous backstage, but we didn't have a dressing-room as such, so we used to get ready wherever we could, generally either in the styling area or in a room if we could get one. Then we'd go and wait in the corridor to go on stage. We don't yet have a proper pre-stage ritual because we haven't been together that long, but I'm sure we will in the future.

Liam: We'd all get into the zone in our own little way. I'd close my eyes and jump around a bit. A bit like a boxer does before a match.

Louis: My only ritual was wearing stripes like a sailor.

Zayn: We didn't really get nervous until we were just about to go on stage, because before that we'd all be chatting. Then it would hits us that 18 million people were about to see us live.

Louis: But once I was on stage I'd instantly go into a completely different mindset. I didn't think about anything, I'd just do it.

opposite page

Louis waits to go out on stage

Liam: When you're singing, you're kind of on autopilot. You just do it, and if you've done the practice, it comes naturally. When I came off stage I usually couldn't remember a single bit of the performance. It was a blur.

The Beatles week was fantastic for me because I'm a massive fan. Although the song we did was an oldie, 'All You Need Is Love', we really

tried to make it feel current. It was a complicated performance for us, full of harmonies and ad-libs, but it was the sort of performance that I think you'd expect from a top boyband. We were feeling the pressure a bit, but we still felt we could go out there and nail it.

Zayn: Niall and I were gutted when Dannii said we struggled with the backing vocals, because we were doing our best. She also said we needed to work as a group, when we thought we were already doing that. I guess she just saw room for improvement. Louis really liked the performance, though, and made a reference to 'the fab five singing the fab four', which was pretty cool. Liam loved that.

Week 8

Harry: We performed the Help for Heroes song, 'Heroes', on the Week 8 show, and it was such an amazing thing to be a part of. I think we all felt really privileged.

Liam: We had a great day filming the video. It was our first one ever, which made it even more special. Then we got to go down to Headley Court in Surrey and meet the soldiers.

Zayn: We had such an amazing day meeting these men who have all been through so much yet have remained so positive and genuine.

Louis: We get overtired and stressed sometimes, because we're working long hours, but meeting the soldiers put it into perspective and reminded us just how lucky we were.

Liam: They've been through such traumatic things and yet they were still happy, and it makes you think that anyone can be happy.

Niall: It was amazing appearing on a number-one single, but it was so much more special because of the cause for which we were doing it.

Harry: We did an interview for Radio One to introduce the single when it went to number one, and it was only afterwards that we realised what a big deal it was.

Louis: Week 8 was rock week, and for the first time we had to sing two songs. 'Summer of '69' is one of my favourite songs, it's a classic that's always playing in clubs and at house parties, and for Niall and me our performance of it was our favourite so far. I liked performing 'You Are So Beautiful' as well, but 'Summer of '69' was just so much fun.

Liam: I think we had really fantastic songs in Week 8, and it was great singing 'You Are So Beautiful' because we just got to stand there and sing, with no gimmicks. It was a totally stripped-back performance. We got really good feedback from the judges as well.

Zayn: Louis said we were going to be the next boyband, which was great because obviously it's what we were aiming for. And even though Simon was our mentor and he's really nice, we would hold our breath each week wondering what he was going to say, and we were always relieved when he said positive things.

Harry: He has sometimes said to his own acts in the past, 'That wasn't good enough.' We hadn't been in that situation yet or seen that side of him, and we didn't want to. We didn't get many bad comments overall, so it was all good.

this page

Niall performing

opposite page

The boys visit
Headley Court

Niall: We were always worried about going home on the Sunday, but that week more than ever we didn't want to go home. The semi-final was within touching distance, and we would have been gutted if we'd been in the sing-off and gone.

Liam: Our name was the last to be called out as safe that week as well, which always made things that bit more stressful. Even though you were through safely, if you'd been called last you still felt as if you'd only just scraped through.

BECOMING STARS

The Semi-final

Liam: Week 9 wasn't the easiest for us, because Zayn had to take some time off for a family matter, and Harry had been ill. So things didn't quite run as smoothly as we'd have liked.

Harry: I was feeling properly awful. I'd been asleep during rehearsals the previous Monday, and then I'd had to leave early on the Friday to go and see a doctor. It was the worst week I could have got ill. It had already happened a couple of times during the competition, so maybe I wasn't fully recovering in-between.

Niall: The rest of us lads pulled together and supported Harry and Zayn as much as we could, and luckily we were so tight as a group by then that we got it together in the course of Saturday when we rehearsed again. We all woke up at 8am to put in extra time.

Louis: I don't think it helped that Harry was outside in the snow a lot, trying to hit us all with snowballs. I reckon that's why he got ill; it was punishment.

Harry: Being cold does not give you a throat infection!

Niall: He was also trying to pelt us through a window, which wasn't very clever.

Louis: We went bowling that week as well, which was such a laugh. I was the best, obviously.

Harry: How come I won then?

Niall: We also got to go to another premiere, this time of *The Chronicles of Narnia*. That was a good crack.

Liam: It was snowing in Leicester Square, so it felt like we'd just walked through the wardrobe into the actual Narnia. And it was great seeing some of the fans and having photos taken with them.

Zayn: Filming the video for what could become our winners' single was a real eye-opener for me. I remember thinking, 'This can't take that long, it's only a short video.' How wrong I was! We'd already filmed the video for the Help for Heroes single, so we did know a bit of what to expect, but this was totally different because it was just us. Now when I watch music videos or TV shows I realise how long it takes to do even the smallest thing, so it's kind of ruined things in a way, but also given me a really good insight into how it all works.

opposite page

Zayn celebrates making it through to the final

Harry: It was an amazing experience. We loved getting to be in our own video. It was something we'd dreamt about and we had such a laugh on the day. We were all quite tired and some of us had been a bit unwell, and it had also been snowing so it was freezing, but it picked us all back up again and we had a brilliant time.

Liam: Saturday night's performance was really good for us. We'd been working hard on the song all week but, to be honest, because of everything that had been going on, we were worried. So we were relieved that we pulled it off. 'Only Girl in the World' was wicked to perform.

Louis: It was great to bust a few dance moves as well.

Harry: We wanted to do our best and have a laugh on stage for 'Only Girl in the World', and then for our second song, 'Chasing Cars', to try and prove ourselves vocally.

Zayn: It was weird to think it could be the last time we performed on *The X Factor* stage. We were all desperate to get to the finals by then. Of course, everyone in the competition was.

Niall: We had a mixed reaction from the judges about 'Only Girl in the World', and Simon and Cheryl even exchanged a few words about it. But, overall, nice things were said and they told us they hoped we were in the final. So did we!

Liam: When Simon said that he was proud of us, that was such a great moment. We were all smiling like maniacs.

Louis: We were so incredibly happy not to be in the sing-off on the Sunday night. But it was really sad to see Mary go. We'd had a good laugh with her in the competition.

Harry: When Dermot called our names and said we were through, I don't think any of us could believe it. We were in the final. The *final*!

opposite page

Louis and Rebecca coming to terms with the fact that they've made it through to the final

The final

Niall: Week 10 was just mad. We were all so excited about being in the final that I think we were all on a total high. Then when we got to do home visits it was amazing. Sadly we couldn't go to Ireland to see my family because of the heavy snow, but we went everywhere else. And we did a live TV broadcast to Ireland, which was brilliant fun.

Louis: We went back to my old school in Doncaster and we could not believe the support we got. People were cheering for us and shouting our names. We loved it!

Harry: We also went back to Cheshire to see my mum and stepdad and have champagne and cake. My stepdad told the boys they were all family now, and that was so nice because we are all so close. These guys are like my best mates now.

Zayn: Later on, we went to HMV in my home town of Bradford and did a signing for fans. It's mad to think that's where I used to shop, and we were back there taking over the place. So many people came to see us and to get that reaction was just …

Liam: Amazing! Then Simon came and joined us and we did a gig in Wolverhampton, where I'm from. Everyone was chanting our names and there were police holding people back. Simon told us that it had been an absolute pleasure working with us and I can tell you we were buzzing!

Harry: Simon seemed really proud of us, which felt amazing because we've got so much respect for him. The gig went brilliantly and gave us just a small taste of what our lives could be like, and we didn't want that to stop. It made us even more determined to show what we could do.

previous pages

Filming the video for what would have been their winners' single

Louis: When the Saturday arrived we were ready for it. We were nervous, but we couldn't wait. That was the moment we'd been working towards for so long.

Niall: It was such a laugh doing the group song, 'What a Feeling', because some of the other contestants came back and it was great to see Aiden and Belle Amie and everyone.

Liam: Our first solo song was Elton John's 'Your Song' and it was properly festive with snow and everything. We had a group hug at the end and we were all feeling quite emotional.

Zayn: Afterwards, Louis said he hoped we would be back on the Sunday and talked about the hysteria we were causing, which was dead funny, and both Cheryl and Dannii said they'd love to see us go through.

'Simon said he'd loved working with us and that we'd proved ourselves as individual singers.'

Harry: When Simon said he'd loved working with us and that we'd proved ourselves as individual singers, it meant so much to us. It's what we'd always set out to do.

Louis: I'm still in total shock that we got to perform with Robbie. He is my absolute hero and an international superstar, and I could not get my head around the fact we'd be singing with him. It's always been my dream to meet him, which I did of course when Take That were on the show, but to be performing with him was just unbelievable.

Liam: We sang 'She's the One' and Robbie genuinely seemed to be enjoying himself. At the end of the song he asked everyone to vote for us, and he even said it was an honour to perform with a band who are at the start of their journey. I guess we must remind him of his early years in Take That. I'd like to think we do anyway – that would be amazing.

Niall: Robbie was such a laugh. He even picked me up at the end and spun me around. I immediately thought, 'I hope someone got a good photo of that!'

Liam: I must have sung 'Angels' in about nine different countries in my life. That's how I started out performing – singing Robbie songs – so for him to potentially be the one who would make it all happen for us in the final was just mind-blowing. He was the person who started it all off for me, so it was magical. I said the first time I entered the show that if I ever got to the final I wanted to perform with Robbie Williams. My dad and I always talked about it, and he knew it was my aim in life to sing with Robbie – and now there he was standing next to me! It made everything else that had happened during the series seem less surreal somehow, because this was just so crazy.

Louis: People say you should never meet your heroes, in case they're not what you expect them to be, but Robbie was everything I expected him to be, and I think we all learnt a lot from him in terms of professionalism and how to conduct yourself as a pop star and a celebrity. He's a perfect example.

Niall: We had to sing in front of him before the show, and he gave us lots of encouragement. And of course we had important questions to ask him – about women and stuff! He's such a cool guy and said that we were handling everything really well.

opposite page

Backstage with Robbie Williams

Harry: He told us that we've got to keep it together and stick together as a band. It's no secret that he and Gary Barlow had some problems back in the day, and there will obviously always be disagreements and confrontations in bands. But generally if we do have them they last less than five minutes and it's all forgotten. He said that was a very positive thing and it bode well for us in the future.

Liam: With your siblings, if you have a row you just get over it, and Robbie said that we have to enjoy all of the time that we spend together because otherwise we're wasting time. He also told us to be nice to everyone we meet and to stay away from drugs! We met Will.i.am backstage as well – and he called me Li.i.am, which was the coolest thing ever.

Zayn: We met Rihanna for a brief second too, but that second will last us a lifetime. She was incredible. We met so many good celebs over the weeks, but she was breathtaking. And Will.i.am was very cool and such a nice guy.

Louis: Going down to the studios on the Sunday morning of the final was so weird because we all knew that it was the last time we'd leave the house as a part of the competition. They were already moving stuff out of the house as we left, so it looked surreal and not the way we had known it.

Niall: When we got to the studio there were hundreds of girls; the most there'd ever been. I guess it was because the other acts like Take That and Rihanna were there too and the girls were all there to see them.

Harry: The first thing we did when we got there was to rehearse the group number for that night, which was very difficult because it was nine in the morning and we'd only just found out that we were going to do the Take That number. We were chuffed to bits, though. We'd already

performed with Robbie, and now we were getting to perform with the whole of Take That.

Zayn: It was amazing and strange to be on stage rehearsing alongside Take That, and also to see Robbie again after performing with him the previous night. He was still buzzing from that performance, and that made us feel a lot more confident about things. We were all incredibly nervous but totally ready for it.

Liam: We didn't go into the final show expecting to win. It was more a case of 'we've come this far and anything else is a bonus'. Of course we all wanted to win, but we knew how strong the competition was with Matt and Rebecca, as they're both such fantastic people and brilliant singers. Then when we started to get ready for that night, it felt weird. There was a different feeling to it compared with previous weeks. I think people were just so glad they'd got to the final of the competition.

Harry: We were all chatting between us about the fact that one of we three acts was going to win, and I think that eased the tension a lot. We had always got on so well with Matt and Rebecca. Obviously there were a few confrontations in the house at times, but that never happened with us. In fact, I would say that if you had to pick three acts who were best mates it would have been Matt, Rebecca and us.

Niall: We always said from day one that we wanted to be in the final with Matt and Rebecca, so it was amazing that it happened. We knew we had to just do our best. Just before the show the judges walked past us and asked how we were feeling, and we had a good chat with Simon which calmed our nerves a bit. It's funny that the same song, 'Torn', ended up being our first and last performance of the series – it seemed we'd come full circle somehow.

previous pages

The semi-finalists

opposite page

The band rehearse for the final show

Liam: We had to battle a bit to get to perform 'Torn', but we felt it was the right song for us to do. I'd never felt so calm going on to a stage as I did when we sang that. We knew the song and it was our last moment on the show, so we all just went for it. The minute we came off stage I knew we'd done our absolute best and there was nothing more we could do. If we went out at that moment, then so be it.

Zayn: Before we went out to hear the final decision, we were standing backstage with Simon, and he said that if we won he would take us on holiday to Barbados. He asked if we thought we'd get through, and we said yes – because we had to think positively. A few minutes later, when we walked off the stage having been told we were out of the competition, Liam turned to Simon and said, 'No chance of that holiday then?' and Simon burst out laughing! That was a funny moment, and it was good to have a bit of a laugh about it, but I was so disappointed.

Louis: After we found out we hadn't made it to the final two we were gutted, there's no denying it. But we did also feel proud of ourselves. It was just the way it was meant to be. We'd made it to the final three of all of the acts, and not many people get to do that. It was a horrible feeling – everyone's there to win – but Rebecca is one of the sweetest girls we'd ever met, and Matt is such a great bloke, so they deserved to be there. They're both really talented.

Harry: All series we kept looking back on what we'd achieved, and when we looked right back to that first performance as a five-piece band in Spain we knew we'd come such a long way. From five lads who never expected to get through to the Judges' Houses section, to eventually making the final three ... We were the only act put together during *The X Factor* ever to reach the final three, and that's a nice little title for us to have, but I was still absolutely gutted.

Liam: As soon as we got off stage Harry was beside himself, but we all had to go up to the ITV2 studio to be interviewed, so I was trying to keep things together. Zayn went off for some time on his own and Harry went to see his mum, and then someone else came up and asked us to do a press interview, which I ended up doing on my own because everyone else was so upset. I was trying to get on with things, but it was really hard.

Louis: We were saying that we couldn't imagine how Rebecca and Matt were feeling, knowing they were down to the final two. It was scary enough getting down to the final three. And when that music starts playing and you have to wait so long to hear whether or not you're through it feels like a lifetime. It must have been terrifying for them to have to go through all of that. It must have felt like days. There's nothing more nerve-racking than being on that stage, hearing everyone screaming, and desperately wanting to know the outcome.

Zayn: After the final, we all had to go back to the house to collect our belongings, and we spent the final evening there. Then we went and stayed in a hotel, as we had some gigs set up and other things to do over the following days. We were all sad not to be in the competition any more, but at the same time all of that pressure was off and we were going to enjoy having more freedom to choose where we went and what we performed. When you're in the show the process is actually pretty tough, and every day is tightly scheduled, but once we were out of it things were very different and less regimented.

Harry: What you see on TV is only part of what actually goes on. We may have been on stage performing just for a few minutes each weekend, but behind the scenes we were rehearsing non-stop and everything was very carefully planned, so it was nice to be doing some totally different things. Especially as we were all so excited about what the future would bring, and getting out there and seeing fans at gigs. We had a good chat at the house and it made us all feel better.

Liam: We were expecting to be on a massive low after the show, but actually there were so many things going on and we had such a good team around us that we managed to pick ourselves back up and have a laugh and look to the future. The support we got on things like Twitter was also a massive help, as it made us realise that we could carry on after the show.

'The support we got on things like Twitter was also a massive help, as it made us realise that we could carry on after the show.'

Zayn: The fans were just incredible and they still are. They've stuck by us, and we got so many messages on Facebook and Twitter telling us that they wanted us to stay together. And then what would have been our winners' single somehow got leaked, and even though it's not official it means that people are still listening to our music. We love the song, and I still feel overwhelmed when I remember we've made our own single and that it's online.

Niall: Getting to record the track was such a massive moment for us. We already felt like a proper band, but that took things to a whole new level. Now we want to get back into the studio and get cracking on our album.

The future

Niall: We always knew that, even if we didn't win *The X Factor,* we would stay together as a band and would try and make it however we could. In a way we've got even more to prove because of the fact that we didn't come first. But we did prove that we could make the band work within a very short space of time. It was us who put all the work in and did all the preparation before Judges' Houses, and we put everything into each week of the competition. Now we have so much more that we want to achieve.

Zayn: The way we found out that we had got our record deal was a true *X Factor* moment. We went for a chat with Simon and he said really seriously, 'I've made a decision.' Then there was a long, dramatic pause, at the end of which he said he was going to sign us! Harry burst into tears and the rest of us had our heads in our hands or just sat there open-mouthed. It was such a crazy moment.

Harry: We were all sitting there, desperate to know our future, and when Simon said those words we were all stunned but so, so happy. It made everything even more worth it, if that was possible. That was what we wanted to hear more than anything else in the world.

Liam: Sitting in front of Simon Cowell and being told you have a record deal is amazing. Bands up and down the country dream of that every day, and in those few moments it became a reality. But we couldn't tell anyone for a little while because we had to have some meetings first to sort everything out.

Louis: When I did tell my parents, they were so thrilled for us all. I think they were in as much shock as we were. The papers were already speculating that we'd been signed, so in a way it was already out there, but it was all guesswork. We didn't actually know until we heard it from

Simon's mouth. It was never, ever a given. A lot of people don't get signed, so we really didn't know.

Niall: We've got a lot of work ahead of us, but we're more than ready for it. We keep getting given schedules for gigs and things, which makes it all feel so real. We got given one recently that had recording dates on, which means that very soon we'll be going into the studio to start recording our music. When we all saw that written down we were hugging each other and couldn't stop smiling. We're so close to achieving what we want.

Harry: We showed so many different sides of ourselves on *The X Factor* and played around with a lot of sounds, and we're looking forward to doing more of that when we're recording the album. And of course we've got *The X Factor* tour to do, which is going to be absolutely amazing. We were looking forward to that the whole time we were in the competition. Liam is the sensible one, so he's going to have to keep us all in check, because we are hoping to have a few parties here and there.

Zayn: We're really looking forward to seeing all the other acts from the show and having a laugh, but we will also be taking it seriously. One day we want to be doing our own tour as One Direction, so while we're planning to have a lot of fun, we're seeing the tour as a really big learning experience too.

Liam: We feel like the future is now wide open for us and we never know what's going to happen next, which is what makes it so exciting. We look at other bands and we've seen how successful they've been. We want some of that for ourselves, and we're willing to work as hard as we need to in order to achieve it. Bring it on!

It's all about the fans

Louis: At the end of the day, we wouldn't be here now if it wasn't for the fans who voted for us. We've received letters and been given some amazing pictures that people have drawn. They've made such an effort. When you arrive somewhere and people are cheering and shouting your name … anyone would love it.

Liam: People stood outside the studios and the house in rain and snow, sometimes until two in the morning. They'd find out where we were and then come and see us. They're so dedicated, and we used to feel awful when we weren't allowed to go out and see them. Sometimes security wouldn't let us go out and say hello, which was frustrating, as we love spending time with them.

Zayn: Some mad things have happened. One girl tried to put her mobile phone into Harry's coat pocket. And it was an iPhone! When he asked what she was doing she said the idea was that if he walked off with her phone he would have to meet up with her the following day to give it back. She was willing to risk losing her phone just so she could see him again!

Liam: People always ask us if we'd date a fan and we definitely would if we met the right girl. It's all about what the person is like, fan or no fan. If they're a nice person and they're pretty, then why not?

Harry: We feel like we're five of the luckiest boys in the world and we just want to say a huge thank you to all the fans. This is just the beginning!

Niall: It was you who got us here, and we won't ever forget that!

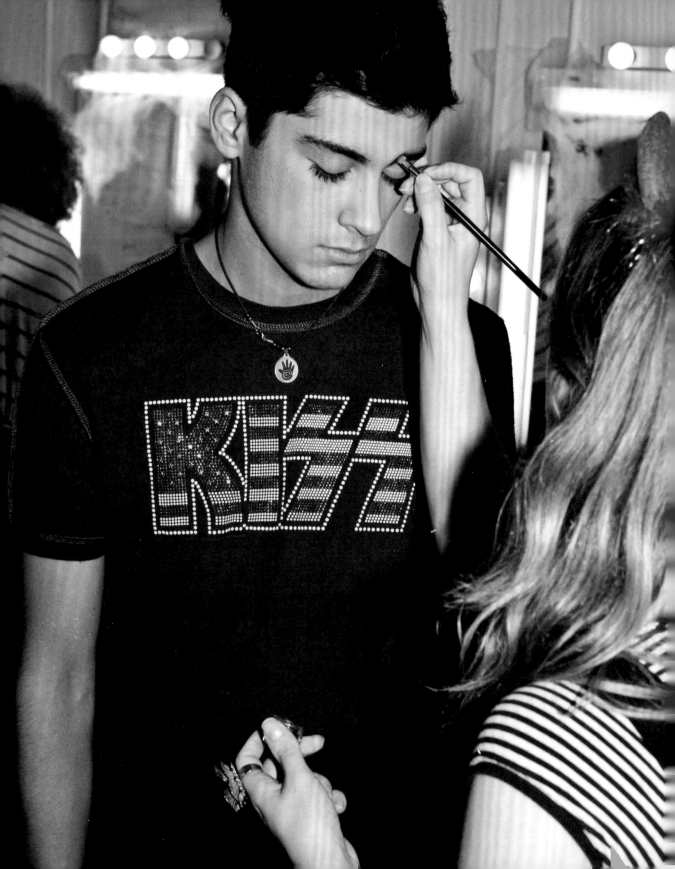

Thanks

We'd like to thank everyone we've worked with over our time on *The X Factor*. We feel that we made many friends on our way. We'd especially like to thank our mentor Simon Cowell, Savan Kotecha, Alison Barker, Tim Byrne, Tyler Brown, Richard 'Biff' Stannard and Brian Friedman for helping us with creative choices and great advice. Mark Sidaway, Richard Holloway, Andrew Ilinares, Jonathan Bullen, all camera and sound crew, all prop crew, special-effects crew and floor managers, Becki Nerves and anyone else for making the show happen. Thanks to everyone from Modest! Management, Richard Griffiths, Harry Magee, Ben Evans, Annecka Griffiths, Georgie Gibbon, Natalie Vassileiou and Will Talbot. Thanks to Adam Reed and Paul Percival, Neil and all at Percy and Reed. Everyone in make-up, Liz, Carol, Jasmina, Kristina, Adam and Cathy. A special thanks to Trudi Lemarie for helping us with styling and creative advice. Thanks to everyone at Fountain Studios including the receptionists who never failed to greet us with a smile, all security and Colin and the Fountain canteen staff. A big thank you to Katie Hobbs, Rob Davies, Helen Bonoah, Josh Jacobs, Joe Street and Claire 'bradders' Bradley for living with us and helping us along. Also thanks to all the runners, you know who you are :). Thanks to Michelle Foreman, Mark Wildash, Carolyn Abatcheta, Pete Ogden and Paul Jones for helping us create some brilliant VTs. Thank you to Dermot O'Leary and Konnie Huq for being so lovely to work with, on and off screen. Everyone at ITV2 and Tim Dean and Gareth Burkit, thank you so much. Thank you to all the researchers, Rebecca Morris, Louis Toplis. Thanks to Tim Gethin, Mark Baker and Diccon Ramsay. Thank you to Sonny and Ann-Marie at Syco. Thank you also to Louis Walsh, Dannii Minogue, Cheryl Cole, Katy Perry and Nicole Scherzinger. Another thank you goes out to Sarah Chelsom who coped with our demand for more tickets, thank you so much. Thank you to all Addison Lee drivers. Also, we feel it's time to say a big thank you to our fans, everyone who voted, waited outside the studio for us...we appreciate every single thing you have done for us. And for everyone who understands, we send out a huge, huge thank you to our old friend.............bag man.

Harry: Firstly a huge thank you to all my friends and family for all the support you've given me throughout my whole experience. A special thanks to my mum and to my dad. Thanks to Katie Hobbs for being my researcher from the start, I owe you a lot. Thanks to my sister Gemma for supporting me. And a final thank you is to my four band-mates...Niall, Liam, Zayn and Louis, I thank you for making this experience what it has been. Again Louis, I thank you for providing me with someone I could always talk to. Thank you everyone, you all mean so much. x

Niall: It's been an amazing experience and I would like to thank my friends and family for staying loyal to me...sorry if I have forgotten anyone...you know who you are!

Liam: I'd like to thank my parents and my family for being so supportive through it all, helping me keep on track with the dream I wanted to achieve and never giving up throughout the last two years. My *X Factor* team Simon Cowell, Tim Byrne, Ali Baker, Savan Kotecha and Tyler Brown for all of their hard work – I really couldn't have done it without them. My old management Ronnie Robinson and Paul Bailey for everything they did to start me off and for being fantastic friends and turning stressful situations into very fun times. My best friends Hannah, Andy, Martin and Hattie for being on the other end of the phone whenever I needed them and helping keep a smile on my face. Danielle Peazer for making me happy through the last few weeks, keeping me grounded and listening to all my problems. Thanks to Jamie for many fun times, always believing in me and helping out where possible. All our researchers – Rob Davis, Helen Banoah, Claire Bradders, Katie Hobbs and Josh Jacobs for helping us get on with it but still making it fun. Louis Tomlinson, Niall Horan, Zayn Malik and Harry Styles – we all did this together and were there for each other through it all. To anyone I have missed I apologise but I appreciate anything you ever did for me.

Louis: I've had a fantastic experience during my time on the show so I would like to take the time to thank the people who have made it extra special.

I wouldn't be where I am today without Simon Cowell, Louis Walsh and Nicole Scherzinger who all put me through my first audition.

Big thanks to Tyler Brown for helping me through the initial stages of the competition and to Ali Barker who deserves a massive thank you on a professional *and* personal level; god knows how you put up with five boisterous and testosterone-filled teenagers but you did tremendously. Tim Byrne you have put hours and hours into making everything we do 'just right' and offering continuous support. Savan Kotecha you helped me and the boys come on leaps and bounds with our vocal ability and you are also the creator of 'Vas Happening Boys' soon to be a number 1 hit I'm sure! Big up to Tom and congratulations on getting the job! ('Keep wearing the TOMS'). Biff, you have produced some unbelievable tracks for us and we wouldn't have got here without the right production, also on that note thank you to Ray and Nigel for the tracks we worked on together.

Brian Friedman, thank you for helping us 'move' around the stage and for directing such fantastic staging. Sid, thanks for putting up with my 'great escape'. A huge thank you to Trudi Lemarie for helping me to fill my wardrobe and being like a mother to me (a really young one at that). You didn't once moan or complain about our crazy antics.

Helen Banoha, thanks for always being there for me throughout the competition, you were my original researcher and have helped me since the day we had that first phone call. Thanks to Katie Hobbs for going into an uncontrollable state of laughter pretty much every minute of every day, Rob Davies for being one of the 'lads' and participating with the usual male banter, Josh Jacobs for fantastic magic ability, Joe Street for looking after my injured foot and being a great friend and to Claire 'Bradders' for being an absolute babe and looking after me when I've needed it.

Modest! Management have all been fantastic – special thanks to Richard, Harry, Ben and of course Annecka. Thank you to 'Interactive Dave' for making some epic online moments such as 'megamind' and 'question time'.

Many thanks to all the fans for supporting us throughout the competition and giving us the strength to go out every Saturday and Sunday. All you lovely people have made this whole competition that extra bit more enjoyable.

To my Mum, without whom I quite literally wouldn't be here, thank you for always loving and supporting me and for making me who I am today. I love you very much and I hope to make you very proud. Dad, you're not bad either......I'm joking, thank you for all your help and 'fantastic' Dad jokes.

Thank you to the rest of my family and friends, especially both sets of grandparents, my great-nan Olive, my Aunty Rach, Stan and Hannah. I would also like to thank Edna and Leonard who were my great-grandparents and who always believed in me throughout their lives. I love you all dearly.

Finally, I wouldn't be sat writing this if it wasn't for four very special people to me: Harry Styles, Niall Horan, Zayn Malik and Liam Payne, I really cannot thank you enough. I've loved every minute of this experience.

Thank you so much guys.

Zayn: I want to thank my Mum for getting me out of bed that day and making me audition when I didn't want to go because it was too early in the morning!!! And Simon Cowell for putting in me in this group and giving me this opportunity even after I refused to dance at Bootcamp. By the way Simon, I'm a great dancer ;-)

I want to thank Tyler for being the sixth member of One Direction, Savan for making every day fun and exciting, Ali for being a great support and being a rock throughout the competition (and for helping me write this), Tim for his pep talks and for having faith in the group from the very start and Biff for making amazing tracks and making us look good.

Thanks to Trudy for giving me loads of clothes, loads of hi-tops and just being an all-round nice woman. I would like to thank *The X Factor* glam squad for making me look half-decent on the show and nothing like I look first thing in the morning!

I want to thank Hobbsy, Bradders, Joe Street, Rob, Josh, and Helen for making this experience a great one and the entire production team at TalkbackThames for everything they have done for me.

Thanks to all at SYCO and Modest!

Liam, Harry, Niall and Louis, 'my Brothers from another Mother' – 'vos apnin boys?!' I intend to remain friends with you for the rest of my life...

One Direction fans, thanks for supporting us from the very start and for coming to the studio every week and appreciating five complete idiots!

And last but by no means least, thanks to my beautiful baby sisters, who I miss more than anything when I'm away from home. My Dad, my 'five other Mothers' aka my aunties and the rest of my family and friends – you know who you are :-)

Simon Harris

Simon Harris is a renowned fashion photographer who regularly shoots editorial pieces for prestigious magazines, including *ID*, *Grazia*, *Drama*, *POP*, *Arena Homme Plus*, *Attitude*, *Perfect*, *Arise*, *Sunday Times Style* and *The Times*. Simon also photographs for international fashion designers, such as Vivienne Westwood, Christopher Kane and Issa. A long-standing member of *The X Factor* family, Simon has shot albums, singles and editorial campaigns for Olly Murs, Shayne Ward, Alexandra Burke, Jedward and Joe McElderry. 'It was an incredible experience working on *The X Factor* books,' says Simon. 'I'm a massive fan of the show – it draws every emotion from the viewers and the artists both onstage and off. To be immersed in the bubble of *The X Factor* for so many months has been a privilege and a rollercoaster experience. For the book, I wanted to capture the excitement, drama and emotion as well as all those intimate moments that are so fascinating and make the show what it is. I hope this book gives readers a further glimpse into the world of *The X Factor* and the amazing people who make it happen.'

HarperCollins*Publishers*
77–85 Fulham Palace Road,
Hammersmith, London W6 8JB

www.harpercollins.co.uk

First published by HarperCollins*Publishers* 2011

10 9 8 7 6 5 4 3 2 1

One Direction are represented exclusively by Richard Griffiths and
Harry Magee for Modest! Management

The X Factor is a trademark of FremantleMedia Ltd and Simco Ltd.
Licensed by FremantleMedia Enterprises www.fremantlemedia.com

© 2010 FremantleMedia Ltd and Simco Ltd

Principle photography © Simon Harris.
Images on pp 4, 34, 37, 38, 41, 43, 46/47, 50, 53, 55, 64, 66/67,
69, 70/71, 82/83, 86, 88, 98, 109, 135, 137, 142/143, 162 ©
FremantleMedia Ltd and Syco.
Special thank you to Ken McKay for the support photography.
Personal photographs on pp 19, 20, 22, 23, 25, 26, 27, 29, 30, 32, 33
courtesy of the authors.

A catalogue record of this book is available from the British Library

ISBN 978-0-00-743230-1

Printed and bound in Great Britain by Butler Tanner and Dennis Ltd,
Frome, Somerset